Sun
on a
Web

Written by Michèle Dufresne

PIONEER VALLEY EDUCATIONAL PRESS, INC.

Look at the **web**.

Spiders spin webs to trap bugs.
Some webs hang high in the trees,
and others are low in the grass.

4

Some spiders spin webs that go across rivers. These webs can be 80 feet long!

The **sun** is on the web.
When the sun hits a web, the web shines like glass.

Look at the bug.
The bug is on the web.

Bugs can get stuck in sticky webs. The spider feels the web shake when this happens.

The bug is wet.

Dew and rain can make webs and bugs wet. Wet webs shine even more!

Wag! Wag! Wag!
The bug wags.

Some bugs, like moths and flies, flap or wiggle fast to try and get free from a web.

The web wins!

Spider silk is strong for its size—stronger than steel by weight! Most insects do not escape from a spiderweb.

glossary

web

sun

wag